My name is...
Vincent van Gogh

Original title of the book in Spanish: *Me llamo...Vincent van Gogh*
© 2004 Parramón Ediciones, S.A.,—World Rights
Published by Parramón Ediciones, S.A., Barcelona, Spain

Name of the author of the text: Carme Martín
Name of the illustrator: Rebeca Luciani

Translated from the Spanish by Eric A. Bye, M.A.

Project and Production: Parramón Publishing
Editorial Director: Lluís Borràs
Editorial Assistant: Cristina Vilella
Text: Carme Martín
Illustrations: Rebeca Luciani
Graphic Design and Layout: Zink Communications, Inc.
Production Director: Rafael Marfil
Production: Manel Sánchez

All inquiries should be addressed to:
Barron's Educational Series, Inc.
250 Wireless Boulevard
Hauppauge, New York 11788
www.barronseduc.com

ISBN-13: 978-0-7641-3394-7
ISBN-10: 0-7641-3394-2

Library of Congress Catalog Card No.: 2005929513

Printed in Spain

9 8 7 6 5 4 3 2 1

Hello...

I was a little of everything throughout my life: art dealer, preacher in a mining region, language teacher, bookseller... but above all, my real passion was painting. Colors are really great; you can do with them much more than you think, and since paintbrushes come in different sizes, there is a limitless number of possible brushstrokes. When you hold the brush, your hands can move in circles, from top to bottom, or in a spiral pattern. That way, light illuminates the painting and it can express all the forces of nature. When I discovered that, I realized that this was my reason for living: painting what you see and how you feel it!

People used to call me the "red-headed crazy man." The business about the hair is pretty clear, since I was born with reddish, wavy hair. But the "crazy" part is something else. The people around me didn't understand my way of thinking, living, and painting, for I sold only one painting in my life—although now my works are the most highly sought-after at art auctions! Newspapers and television frequently discuss my drawings, oil paintings, and watercolors, and art counterfeiters try to imitate me. In Holland, my native country, they have created a foundation and a museum under my name, they organize commemorations in my honor, and they write countless articles and books in which they try to explain my paintings and my style. So who's the "crazy" one here?

Big Eyes and Red Hair

I was born on March 30, 1853, in a small town in the Dutch region of the Brabant called Groot Zundert. I was a long-faced baby with big, bright eyes and reddish, wavy hair, and I was the pride of my parents. They were named Theodorus and Anna Cornelia; they were two good people with a very rigid and conservative nature. My father, a strict Protestant minister, taught me discipline and to put will and effort into everything I did, but I never got along with him very well, and we frequently argued. My mother, who was sweet and understanding, taught me to love nature and works of art; she also supported me in my decisions and made peace when my father and I were fighting.

I was the oldest of six brothers and sisters: Theodorus, Cornelius, Anna, Elizabeth, and Wilhelmina. My favorites were Theo and Wil, because they too were interested in art, and they always followed my progress with the paintbrushes. Wil was the smallest of the girls, and she liked to draw as much as I did. When I was living at my parents' house we would go on long walks together in the country. Theo was four years younger than I was, and he always encouraged me to paint and be a good artist.

In school the teachers thought that I was a child with deep, observant eyes, quiet but with a lively intelligence. I didn't like any subject in particular, although I did well at languages, like many other Dutch people. My amusement was to walk alone through the neighboring fields and roads, catch colored insects, collect fragrant plants and flowers, and draw the animals and landscapes that I saw using pencil and charcoal.

My First Contact with Art

At the age of sixteen I left school to work as an art dealer, buying and selling paintings at Goupil and Company. With my salary I could help my family, since my father didn't earn much money as a Protestant minister. Goupil and Company was one of the most important art galleries in all of Europe at that time. It had branches in The Hague, Brussels, London, and Paris, and since my uncles Cent and Cor worked there, they managed to get me a position as an assistant in the gallery at The Hague. This was my first contact with the canvases of the Dutch Realist painters and the paintings of the French Naturalist school.

After a short while, my brother Theo also started working for Goupil and Company, but in its Brussels branch. Great! Now we had more things in common! Ever since the previous summer we had enjoyed spending lots of time together in our parents' house. We would spend our days talking about painters, books, our hopes, what each of us would be when we grew up...

Luckily, Theo and his wife kept all our correspondence, and many years later, their son, Vincent Willem van Gogh, gave the letters to the van Gogh Foundation, which was created in my honor in 1931 in Amsterdam. Experts now say that the letters are an important tool for understanding my art. But let's not get ahead of ourselves...

Since I was a good worker, when I turned twenty they transferred me to the London gallery, which was much more important. Thank goodness! I was getting tired of the common, middle-class customers and their bad taste.

I was dazzled by the English capital; I took long walks along the Thames River and visited the city's fabulous museums and galleries. It was exciting to walk in its cloudy, rainy climate. Everything I experienced made me want to draw. Also, I fell in love with a girl for the first time, and love filled me with life and optimism. We talked about art, literature, and we laughed. Eugeine made me believe that she loved me, but unfortunately she refused to marry me.

My failure at love caused me to experience a bad time in my life; I was sad and out of sorts. Everything looked gray to me, and I frequently vented my bad mood on the customers at the gallery. My supervisors at Goupil and Company wanted to fire me because of my behavior, but my uncles prevented that and I was transferred to the gallery in Paris. My attitude didn't improve much there, either. I could see that this job wasn't for me. I didn't want to deceive the customers, or give them bad advice. My desire was to educate them to sensitivity and good taste with my recommendations about art.

In Search of My Life's Work and Theo

My brother Theo and I exchanged numerous letters—more than six hundred! In the ones I wrote from London, I began to include pencil sketches of the landscapes I saw and the people with whom I associated. That gave Theo the idea that I should become a painter. Me, an artist? I thought my brother was looking too favorably on my drawings. I needed to find some important job, and I didn't think that being an artist was it. I was looking for a job that would help nature, serve others, and give meaning to my life.

I left Paris and returned to England, where I was happy for a while. In Ramsgate I got a job as a language teacher in Mr. Stokes's school. Evidently I didn't do badly, but I was less interested in teaching than in helping the boys with their day-to-day lives. From there I went to another school in Isleworth, where in addition to teaching classes I was an assistant pastor in the town church, and I gave my first sermon. The experience led me to become a great reader of the Bible, and after selling books in the city of Dordrecht for a few months, I returned to my home in Etten so I could explain my new, great goal to my parents: I wanted to become a Protestant pastor like my father.

I needed preparation for this new job, so I went to study theology in Amsterdam. I failed the entrance exams because I didn't know Latin and Greek. They seemed very difficult to me! But since I was very determined and put great effort into all my projects, I refused to give up and took a simple course in Brussels to become a preacher.

Finally, a Chance to Preach!

I was sent to the Belgian mining region of Borinage, in the small village of Wasmes. In my twenty-five years of living this was the first time I had seen poverty so close. It was awful! The miners worked twelve or fourteen hours a day digging coal from deep in the earth. Their salary was almost nothing, and all they had to eat was soup made from bread and potatoes. The whole family, from the youngest children to the adults, helped with the jobs inside and outside the home. They wore the same clothing and the same shoes until they were worn out, and the women stitched and mended pants that were full of patches.

I was ashamed to come from a middle-class family and to be able to eat and get dressed every day. So I gave away my food, my clothing, and my shoes to the neediest people. I lived badly like them so I could feel useful, and I helped them in every way possible.

What despair! I stopped taking care of myself, and I started smoking a pipe so I wouldn't eat so much. After two years, my bad health and my dangerous situation became a worry to my family, especially to Theo, since I wasn't writing him as often. He immediately realized that I wasn't well, even though I tried to hide it.

The only comfort was being able to draw those men, women, and children. I did so in my letters to Theo to show him what the life of the miners was like. In some way, my pencil and charcoal doodles seemed to soften their poverty. I did countless studies of their long, friendly faces, their calloused, bony workers' hands, the hardworking women, the wise elders… It was a hard experience, but it tremendously enriched my character as a person and an artist.

It was clear that being a preacher wasn't right for me either, and I went to spend a few months in Cuesmes, another mining district, to ponder my future. Within myself I yearned for contact with works of art, but it was hard for me to realize that. One day I walked over 24 miles (40 km) to the house of Jules Breton, a painter I admired, but I didn't have the courage to go in. Finally, following the advice of Theo in his most recent letter, I began to do some sketches of mining families I knew. At that time I also developed a taste for copying paintings, such as *The Four Hours of the Day* and *The Sower* by the great realist painter Jean-François Millet, who devoted himself to studying peasants and their customs.

Being alone, close to my beloved nature, fields, and forests, drawing peasants and their daily labor, opened my eyes. Finally, at the age of twenty-seven, I figured out what my mission in life would be.

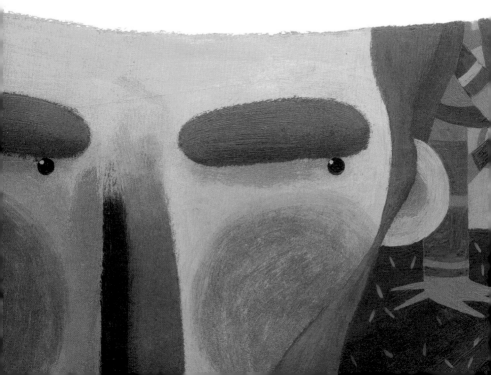

I Want to Be a Painter!

Painting! My dear brother Theo was very happy about my decision. Filled with hope, he sent me money to begin my painting studies, and he recommended a well-known young painter named Anthon van Rappard. Theo had become a friend of his in Paris, and Anthon told him, "If you wish, Vincent can come to my studio in Brussels and I will show him how to draw." My first attempts turned out as expected: my drawings were crude and clumsy, and my lines were rigid and indecisive. That didn't matter, because I knew that I would manage to become a good artist, and my family and friends encouraged me to continue. The following spring I went to the family home in Etten, and my mother helped me set up a little painting studio.

Have I mentioned my fascination with nature? And for the daily work that people do? The Dutch countryside seemed endless, and its earthy and yellowish colors changed according to the crops and the orchards. The peasants would hoe, sow, and harvest from morning to evening, illuminated by different tones of light and shadow.

I was happy and overflowing with energy, and I soon fell in love with my cousin Cornelia, who visited us frequently because she had recently become a widow. Although I demonstrated my determination to marry her, I was rejected by her parents and even by her. I soon became depressed: my second love was gone, my father and I weren't getting along, and I wasn't making progress in my art. Very unhappy and misunderstood, I took Theo's advice and retreated to my art studies. At the end of the year I went to The Hague, the city where our cousin, the famous painter Anton Mauve, lived, for he agreed to be my teacher.

Even Uncle Cor was interested in my progress as an artist, and he hired me to do some views of the port city.

Anton was so kind to me! He gave me my first box of watercolors and taught me how to use and apply colors. At first I did countless studies of still lifes and plaster figures: apples, pitchers, shoes… Then, along with some other painters, we visited picturesque places in the city to draw them.

I wanted to use real flesh-and-blood people as models, but my cousin felt that I should first practice in the studio. The learning seemed to take forever! I was anxious and nervous. One day I got angry with Anton because of his technical inflexibility, and I broke one of the figures in his workshop. That day I decided to set up my own artist's studio and live with a woman I had just met.

My Home with Sien and My First Oil Paintings

Clasina Maria Hoornik was not particularly pretty or young, but she was expecting a baby and she had a small daughter. I met them one day in the street; they earned their living in a bad way, so I took them into my studio and offered them everything I had. As I explained to Theo in a letter, "I believe that any man worth at least his shoe leather would have done the same thing in a similar situation."

Love and tenderness were like a soothing ointment for me. I fell in love with the fragility and the innocence of Sien's daughter— for that was my nickname for her—and Sien's way of facing life. I taught them to pose, and I did many drawings of them, both together and individually. The most famous ones are *The Great Lady* and *Sorrow*. In the first, I created the figure of a white, slender woman grieving in the dark of the night. The second is a moving pencil sketch of Sien. It shows the deep pain of the

nude body of a woman who hides her head in her hands to avoid looking out at the world that mistreats her.

Some people, including my family, thought we were sinners. Nonsense! Is it a sin to be in love? To use our hearts to help people in need? The world is happier when you have someone with you who needs you and loves you. Also, where there are children there is laughter and creativity. They stimulated my imagination, and that's when I began to experiment with oil paints: first with basic colors, and then with mixes. I explained my ambition in one of my letters to Theo: "I want to reach a point where it is said of my work: This man feels deeply and delicately."

After more than a year of intense work, and some arguments with Sien, I was experiencing painful headaches, and I had increasing pains in my teeth and stomach. I became ill, and my father, after being convinced by my good brother Theo, came to get me. It was painful to leave, but I yearned for life in the country, and I was practically out of money...

In the Family Home in Neunen: 250 Paintings!

Before leaving for Neunen, where my parents lived at the time, I traveled to Drenthe, in the north of Holland, at the recommendation of my good friend van Rappard. I spent two months of reflection in the dull countryside among the peasants, with their fieldwork and their simple life. I needed a little calm and to improve my artistic studies.

I was searching for new images and wanted to achieve the genius of the great French realist painter Millet, who specialized in rural subjects. Taking inspiration from his paintings and peasant scenes, I painted several versions of his paintings to perfect my technique. Finally I was returning to the nature I adored!

I was thinking seriously about focusing on painting portraits to earn money, since I hated being an economic burden to Theo. At that time my brother lived in Paris, an extremely expensive city, even for a major art dealer at Goupil and Company. Since it was difficult to locate good, available models for portraits, I thought, "What better model than myself?" I could remain seated for

hours in front of the mirror without complaining, and for free! Throughout my life I did thirty-five self-portraits of very different kinds. At the beginning I depicted myself as a bourgeois man using sweet, warm tones, and my style kept evolving until the last self-portrait at Saint-Remy in 1889, which was positively dazzling.

I spent the next two years in Neunen at the home of my parents. This was a very productive period of my career: more than two hundred works, including oil paintings, watercolors, and charcoal drawings. In part this was due to the love and serenity of my mother. Since she had broken a leg in an accident, she couldn't move for many months. I dedicated myself entirely to her. We spent many hours together; she would read and I would draw next to her the subjects that she liked best: churches with hedges, cemeteries with groves of trees, orchards, people from town… The dominant colors in my palette were the blackish tones typical of the Dutch realist painters.

The Potato Eaters

In March of 1885, at the age of thirty-two, I painted my first large canvas, *The Potato Eaters*, a picture that represented my "Dutch phase"; as the specialists in my works have declared, it is characterized by an unmatched dramatic expressionism.

I'll describe it for you. The Groot peasant family—parents, daughter, and grandparents—is seated around the table, illuminated by a weak light that hangs from the ceiling, for their dinner, which consists of potatoes. They are working people from the Dutch region of Brabant. The peasants have a special, simple beauty, with their patched clothing covered with dust, an odor of grease, potatoes, smoke, and sweat...

You can sense a pure, simple soul behind the weather-beaten faces and the bony hands. They are in a room painted in greens and blues that suggest the outdoors.

I did three versions of the same painting and several portraits of peasants as training studies, for I wanted to achieve mastery of the chiaroscuro technique (the use of light and shade) used by Rembrandt. I was trying to achieve effects of light in darkness, and commented to Theo on my palette of colors: from the white of silver to vermilion red, yellow, ocher, sienna, cobalt blue, and black. I was so satisfied that I wrote him in a letter, "It looks like it's alive." "Congratulations!" he wrote me from Paris, and he sent me a book by the Goncourt brothers, who were French realist writers.

Two months later I was told that my father had died. The news made a deep impression on me, and I couldn't paint for several days. Even though we had never gotten along very well, I grieved the death of the good man my mother loved with all her heart.

I was hearing a lot about the Impressionist "revolutionaries," who had started an art movement against traditional, academic art. It had begun a few years previously in Paris, the cultural capital of Europe ever since the eighteenth century. I mentioned to Theo my desire to live with him to get to know these artists in person. But my brother didn't seem very excited by the idea. I told him, "In order to get something hot you have to go where the heat is; otherwise it's hard to fend off the cold." I was thirty-two years old, and I felt that in some southern European country I would find the warm air necessary for my health and the light essential to my palette of colors. But I didn't convince him... for the moment.

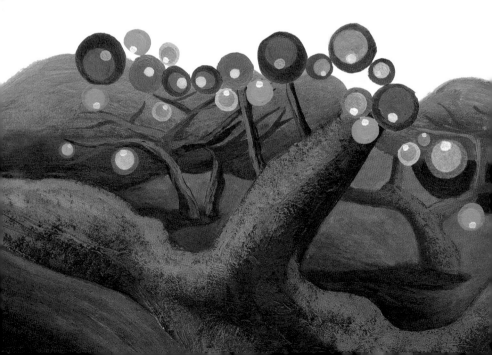

Antwerp and Japanese Engravings

I was ill at ease and wanted a change. I thought, "I'll go to Antwerp to improve my style and see the works of Rubens, whom I admire, in the city museum." When I arrived, I enrolled in the Academy of Art to perfect my technique of painting from a model. And… they put me in with the beginners! The professors were very strict with the rules, too rigid and opposed to experimenting. Therefore, I went to few classes and focused on enjoying the activity in the port of Antwerp. Every day I went from one end to the other, and during my walks through the antique and book shops, I discovered some beautiful Japanese engravings; I loved the power and the grace of the flowers, the delicacy of the Japanese women illuminated by the midday sun, the harmony of their compositions…

I felt that Holland had nothing more to offer me, and I sent a letter to Theo asking him to let me come to Paris with him and meet modernity face to face. I wrote him, "We have spoken a lot about Impressionism by letter, but from Holland it's hard to understand what this movement really means."

Finally... Paris and the Impressionists!

At that time, Paris was a great cosmopolitan city, the artistic and cultural center of all Europe. There were major Universal Expositions, such as the one in 1876, with the participation of various countries from around the world. These were a type of huge fair for cultural, scientific, and commercial exchange in which each participating nation exhibited its technical innovations, new products, and the best of its culture. At one of these fairs, the displays included the color photographic camera and Japanese handcrafts.

Impressionism was born as a great revolution in art within this environment of progress. Traditional paintings were done in closed studios, using artificial light, perfect figures, with proper poses and attitudes, and clean, classical colors. Everything was carefully planned and studied. It wasn't real! In contrast, Impressionist paintings were done outdoors using natural light, with normal people, without poses, with natural facial expressions, and with colors that varied based on the observation of each person and the spontaneous emotion of the moment. Everything was left up to the artist's improvisation, so that this personal freedom created images that were authentic!

The Impressionists were a group of painters united in defense of common ideas of beauty. Manet, Monet, Degas, Renoir, Seurat, and Pissarro, among others, believed in these new ideas, such as painting outdoors, illuminating the new compositions with many brushstrokes and fragments of color, depicting natural subjects... The presentation of their paintings took place at the Nadar gallery exposition, which coincided with the exposition of the official Salon in 1874. The sarcastic columnist Leroy tried to make fun of Monet's painting *Impression: Rising Sun*, of which he declared, "That painting, vague and brutal at first glance, is at the same time the affirmation of an ignorance and the negation of the true and the beautiful." That became the source of the group's name, the Impressionists.

These painters commonly were found at the cafés of Paris, where they discussed technical questions. Pissarro, the eldest, held that, "The warm colors of the palette are the best ones for painting outdoors," and the poetical Monet answered him, "Yes, yes, but especially for painting reflections in the water." And Renoir, the least revolutionary, added, "Still, we mustn't forget open composition..." They all wanted to contribute their own vision of the interplay of the primary (yellow, red, and blue) and secondary (violet, green, and orange) colors, and their special ways of using the brush. Some chose to make dots very close together; others superimposed lines; one broke up each brushstroke; another applied small, curving touches... An endless array of possibilities!

"Surprise, Theo! Shall we meet at the Louvre at noon?" I sent him a note at his work. I was impatient and nervous. Now we wouldn't have to write to one another to explain our experiences and artistic progress to one another. We would speak every day. We would share everything, and I would introduce myself to the Impressionists, the art critics, the gallery owners... Theo would bring me to the famous gatherings in the cafes, to the important art studios, and to the workshops of the famous artists.

A new world of sensations and passions was opening up before my eyes. My two years of living in Paris would be very fruitful: I would learn the trade of being a painter and improve my technique with the help of my friends the Impressionists.

Cormon's Studio

At first, Theo and I lived in his little apartment on Laval Street. There was no room for an artist's studio. Every morning he would go the Goupil and Company gallery, and I, with my hat, my pipe, and my notebook under my arm, would walk through the streets and parks of Paris. I would visit the museums, the art galleries, and the markets. My favorite places were the banks of the River Seine and the Montmartre section, where it was possible to experience life among unconventional, artistic people.

Theo was the best brother anyone could desire: he found a large apartment with a workshop in Montmartre, he brought me to the shop of old Tanguy to buy paints, canvases, and Japanese engravings, and he enrolled me in Fernand Cormon's studio. There I improved my technique in the company of Henri de Toulouse-Lautrec, Georges Seurat, and Paul Cézanne, and I met my friend Émile Bernard, the joker.

Cormon showed us the *cloisonnisme* technique, which consisted of painting large circular surfaces with flat colors and outlining them in black. He encouraged us to bring together all the colors to establish light and symbolize the elements of nature, such as yellow for the radiant sun and red for a setting sun.

I enjoyed experimenting with this technique, especially to increase the expressiveness of my works.

After class, in the afternoons, we would listen to the conversations of the old Impressionists, such as Pissarro and Guillaumin, in the Café Guerbois or the Moulin de la Galette. Pissarro had such experience, and he too was a fan of the Japanese engravings.

He taught me to see the best in them: their images without shadow or sculpting, and the flat, warm light. He also advised me to use light colors and showed me a new way of arranging the elements on a canvas. Guillaumin insisted on the necessity of dividing up the hues of the colors gradually by using small brushstrokes.

We frequently visited the shop of old Julien Tanguy. It was a strange little warehouse of pictures, canvases, and... a huge pile of odds and ends. Mr. Tanguy would sell us everything that artists needed to work. The kind *père*, as we called him, was devoted to getting the pigments, canvases, and brushes that we ordered at good prices. And if we couldn't pay him, he would say, "All right, give me one of your paintings instead and we're even." The shopkeeper would hang them in his front window to sell, or else he would bring them home because he liked them.

To apply the new knowledge I had picked up, I painted the *Portrait of Père Tanguy*. I painted it to express my gratitude to him, since he always put my canvases in the display window. The kind dealer spent hours posing for me, and I always remembered that with fondness. The outline of the figure is simple and vigorous. The background is filled with Japanese engravings. The hues of burnt umber in interlaced brushstrokes of ocher and white create the roughness of the flesh and the strength of the hands.

The Paris Cafés

Theo wrote to our mother, "In his work, Vincent has made perceptible progress and is starting to experience success. He is also in a better mood than before, and the people here like him. I think that if we can continue like this, his financial difficulties will be over and he will be able to fend for himself." In truth, everything seemed to be going along smoothly. I was spending as much time as possible with my new friends while Theo took a trip to Holland for business.

We all liked the animated colors and enjoyed discovering new ways of painting. Paul Gaugin impressed me because of his self-confidence. Émile Bernard's good humor was contagious, and he would calm me down during the heated discussions about painting that took place at the cafés.

Gaugin and Bernard agreed on the symbolic value of color. For example, red for passion, orange and yellow for the sun and warmth, dark blue for a mysterious night, and so forth. Toulouse-Lautrec invited me to drink absinthe—the fashionable drink in the cafés—and spoke to me of his passion for painting women. Seurat kept insisting on the importance of the brushstroke. Cézanne thought that color could express outline, volume, and light, all at the same time.

I turned into a "tireless chatterbox," as Bernard called me, filled with projects. Ah, what dreams! Amazing expositions, artists' colonies in the south of France, a takeover of the public media to educate the masses... I believed that art would improve the world, but I realized that very few were following along with me or understood me. In addition, I discovered quite a lot of intrigue and jealousy among the artists. That environment wasn't for me after all.

Months later, in Arles, I painted *Night Café* to reflect my sensations and emotions of those nights in the cafés.

The colors red and green dominate this painting; they express passion and desolation. The scene shows a few people in a café poorly lit by gaslights. The light vibrates due to separate brushstrokes in a circular pattern. Mysterious objects are immobile in a space of flat colors.

Paris was extremely expensive, some artists disappointed me, and I was bored with always hearing the same things. I wasn't feeling anything new and didn't have any inspiration. In addition, at that time I started arguing with Theo, for he had started going out seriously with his friend's sister, Johanna Bonger, and he wanted to get married. I could tell that I was in the way, and Pissarro and Bernard advised me to move to the south of France, to Provence, in search of bright sunshine. I left my two hundred paintings and about fifty drawings from that period with Theo, but I took along my Japanese engravings, my paints, and an idea: starting an artists' colony.

Arles: the Sun of Southern France

I arrived by train in February of 1888 and rented an apartment near the station. It was still winter, and I didn't find the famous heat and sunlight that I wanted so badly. The first days were very strange, for I felt great pleasure at rediscovering the peace of living alone, but at the same time I longed for the excitement of the cafés in Paris. I resumed my correspondence with Theo to forget our quarrels. I owed him so much! I had already said so in a letter to our sister Wil before arriving here: "If it weren't for Theo, I couldn't complete my work; having his support to count on helps me move forward."

When spring arrived, the white beams of sunlight penetrated the trees in the clean air of Arles and flooded my room with light. At the age of thirty-five I had found paradise, and I painted nonstop. First, I painted my own *Bedroom* to show what my place of rest and tranquillity was like: a couple of chairs and a yellow bed the color of fresh butter, sheets and pillows of lemon yellow, walls of pale violet, an orange wash table, my hat, my pipe, and my paintings on the wall.

I could work all day long outdoors. I liked to study the same subject under different light conditions and from several points of view. So I painted *The Langlois Bridge, The Crau Plain, The Sower, Self-Portrait with Straw Hat...* The style of the Japanese prints was present in my works, and I completely abandoned Dutch chiaroscuro. I painted everything I saw under a boundless sun. The sun in my canvases was like a huge yellow spider, constructed from circular brushstrokes crossed by radial lines.

The fields stretched out forever, and I took pleasure in describing every small detail in the landscape with my brushes: ochers and yellows in the wheat, blues on the hills, and some contrasts in red.

Passionate Sunflowers

The artists in Paris were looking for an art of impression: I was looking for expression, a means for expressing authentic reality, not just appearances. Color was the reflection of my state of mind, applied with increasingly intense and forceful brushstrokes. The canvases were spaces filled with light and color and figures that weren't drawn but modeled with the paintbrush. The sunlight flooded through the window in torrents, and I saw before me the trees, bushes, and flowers of the park. The ardent sunflowers stood out, and I remembered a comment by Gaugin, in his last letter, about a painting he had seen in Paris.

Claude Monet had painted a bouquet of sunflowers in a large Japanese urn. These flowers are the symbol of the sun on the French Mediterranean coast.

I found inspiration in everything. So I did some studies of *Sunflowers* in different shades of orange and yellow, pure expression through color. These are among my most famous paintings. The shades of orange are multiplied until they become greenish hues in the different canvases of the series. These simple flowers all seem different, shaped like balls or with tangled petals. Fragmented brushstrokes are no longer visible— the brushes glide along the canvas in a continuous, strong, and aggressive fashion. The iridescent lines define the shapes of the flowers. Yellow on yellow, orange on orange... I kept applying lots of touches in a frantic, circular rhythm without stopping. The sunflowers turn, and they turn toward the sun!

The Yellow House

My paintings from that time are a reflection of my passion. I was experimenting with the vital force of nature in everything I painted: landscapes, trees, flowers, people... In my letters to Theo and my artist friends, I explained what I was feeling and enticed them with my old project of creating a community of artists. Living together to save expenses, and at the same time exchanging ideas, sharing experiences in the same workshop, putting on exhibitions together... everything we talked about in the cafés of Paris but in a warmer, purer place, with no expensive distractions. At the end of September 1888, I painted *The Yellow House*, the ideal place to lodge my artist friends if they decided to live communally. The only one who was interested in coming was the passionate Paul Gauguin. He had returned from his trip to Martinique and was practically broke. Paul and I shared expenses, with Theo's help, and in exchange we sent him our paintings to sell in Paris.

Those were two complicated months, but they were very creative for both of us. At first, everything worked perfectly. Paul was a good cook, I had a large collection of prints to copy, and I brought him all my favorite landscapes for inspiration. The day we had the most fun was when we challenged one another. Paul asked me, "Can you do your self-portrait by copying my style?" I told him, "Sure! A good painter has to be able to copy any style. How about you? Could you do your self-portrait the way I paint?" So the two of us began to work like crazy, and we didn't eat until we had finished. The joker Paul entitled his *Les Misérables* to poke fun at painters who weren't yet famous, such as the two of us at that time. I entitled mine *Self-Portrait for My Friend Paul*. And we gave each other our paintings as a token of our friendship.

Too bad this nice environment didn't last very long... Gauguin, like me, was a stubborn, passionate lone wolf. One day we visited the museum at Montpellier, and when we returned home, we argued violently about the merit of a painting in the museum. We began yelling without even realizing it. When Paul became aggressive and wouldn't listen to me, I became frightened and threatened him with a knife. Paul, afraid and furious, took off and got on the first train for Paris, then told Theo what had happened. I never remembered what happened after the fight. I remember that I hung around the dark streets of Arles for a while with a bad headache. The next day I woke up in a hospital with my ear bandaged. They told me that I had cut off part of my ear. That was my first major nervous breakdown.

Once I had recovered, I returned to my beloved yellow house with a desire to resume painting. The first days I didn't leave my apartment much, for I felt weak. I copied a few illustrations from my collection, I painted a self-portrait, and I played with color combinations on my palette, but I didn't know if I would ever be the same again. Nothing was clear to me. Some neighbors were afraid of me. Theo was afraid for me, and I was afraid of my growing mental illness... I asked Theo to take me to live in an asylum in Saint-Rémy de Provence.

Starry Night

My life in the asylum at Saint-Paul-de Mausolé, an old convent in the town of Saint-Rémy de Provence, was just what my spirit needed. My health improved quickly, and the surrounding beautiful landscape stimulated my desire to paint. I painted a few portraits and a hundred canvases of the landscape that surrounded us. I exchanged the sunflowers of Arles for scnes of olive trees and cypresses. I wrote to Theo about my fascination with these trees: "The cypresses are as beautiful as an Egyptian obelisk: they looked like dark blades of vibrant energy climbing skyward." My brushes wanted to follow them with winding movements, and I became obsessed with that dizzying rhythm.

I experienced a second breakdown when I tried to poison myself by swallowing paint, and my brushes and palette were taken away from me for a while. My depression had returned with a vengeance. Thus, I could only do pencil portraits of the people nearby and copy engravings from my collection. But they quickly realized that the only way I could get better was by painting outdoors, day and night, and they decided to go with me on my outings with the brushes.

I had always been fascinated with the problem of depicting scenes from nature or cities at night. Night skies filled with stars were my obsession. When I was in Arles, I had made myself a hat surrounded by a crown of lighted candles so I could paint in the middle of a field, or else I would walk through the town and stop beneath the streetlights.

My most famous night sky is called *The Starry Night*; I painted it in oils in June of 1889. The scene depicts a town at night. The houses occupy a small space at the bottom of the canvas. Behind them there is a greenish forest and some bluish mountains. The focus is on the luminous stars, which take up more than the top half of the canvas in a horizontal stripe, along with a shining, golden moon. Everything is filled with a dizzying rhythm produced by the vibrant brushstrokes. The strokes twist and turn, creating spirals with many parallel colors. Cypresses stand out in the foreground and climb up to the deep sky as a counterpoint to the trail of stars shining forth in the dark night.

The twentieth-century school of German expressionists took this painting as a source of inspiration. They said that the use of color, especially black, to transmit feelings and energy expressed the agony of my mind.

Theo told me the good news of the moment: two of my paintings were exhibited in the 1889 Salon of the Independents in Paris, and a journalist praised my style. Shortly thereafter, a lady painter in Brussels bought from Theo the first and only painting of mine that ever sold during my lifetime, *The Red Vineyard*. And I wrote to Theo with other news: I was feeling better and I wanted to live closer to him. My Impressionist friends had recommended a place near Paris—a doctor who was very interested in art lived there.

Doctor Gachet in Auvers-sur-Oise

No sooner said than done! Theo came to get me in February and moved me to the northeast of Paris, to a place called Auvers-sur-Oise. Some other painters, such as Cézanne, also lived there, and there was a hostel near the house of Dr. Paul Gachet, who was to take care of me in the coming months.

First I wanted to spend a few days in Paris to get to know my nephew. Jo and Theo had named him Vincent in my honor! Those days were tense but emotional ones, for I was once again among my old painter friends, and I saw many of my works hanging on the walls in Theo's apartment. I was glad to see them happy, but at the same time I was sad, because I didn't want to be a burden to my dear brother.

I moved into the hostel at Auvers-sur-Oise, and in my first weeks there, I recovered, thanks to the care of a very special man. Paul Gachet was both a doctor and an engraver. He was a good friend of artists in general and of Camille Pissarro in particular, and he immediately took me into his care. It's not that he gave me any special medicine, but his conversations on art and life in general were the best therapy. He insisted that I paint, and I agreed: I created more than eighty paintings in two months!

He was my model in one of them. In the *Portrait of Dr. Gachet* I hoped to show the friendship that bound us together. The figure of this good and friendly man leans against a tabletop. His face rests on one hand, and the other hand holds some of the plants the he used for medicine.

You can detect a certain anxiety in the brushstrokes, in the composition, and in the space that surrounds the figure. The contrasts of pure colors, red and blue, to heighten the expression, reflect internal tension. The doctor wasn't aware of how afraid I was of my illness—although when I set to work with my brushes I seemed to forget it all.

My painting had taken on another rhythm, dominated by unrealistic colors and a preference for ancient buildings, such as *The Church in Auvers*. It represented a Gothic church crumbling among twisting roads, beneath a sky with whirlwinds of blue.

The Last Letter to Theo, July 27, 1890

During the month of July, I again became fond of going out alone into the countryside. The contact with nature seemed to do me good and gave me strength to continue painting. In that area there were great flocks of crows that flew over the fields. The farmers would shoot into the air to frighten them away and keep them from eating the grains. I too used the same system so I could paint them.

One of my last great oil paintings, painted before July 9, 1890, is in fact entitled *Wheatfield with Crows*. It's very special because I didn't apply the color with a brush, but rather with a palette knife so I could spread it out furiously on the canvas. It shows a stormy sky in blacks and blues, eclipsed by purplish clouds at the top of the canvas. The rest of the canvas depicts a huge, orange-yellow wheat field, stirred up by the wind blowing among the stalks. A

road in reddish tones stands out in the middle, and above everything are the dramatic black shapes of the crows' wings.

On July 27, 1890, I went out to the countryside as always. My despair became too much for me, and I shot myself with a pistol. I staggered as I returned to the house. Dr. Gachet notified my brother, and I spent my last night in his arms. The bullet in my body could not be removed. In my hands I clutched my last letter to Theo: "Well, the truth is that we can do no more than make our paintings speak for us. Still, my dear brother, I will always consider that you are something more than a simple seller of artwork by Corot; through me you have contributed to the production of certain canvases that maintain their calm even in disaster." The next day, on July 29, 1890, my lifelong pain ended with my death. My coffin was covered with the sunflowers that I so dearly loved.

My brother Theo died six months later, after suffering a breakdown.

"Let our paintings be the ones to speak…" This is the legacy I leave to the world. I live through my paintings and my correspondence with Theo, Wil, van Rappard, Émile Bernard… The letters are a complete account of my evolution as an artist and my experiences as a human being. Every touch of color in my paintings is a vital moment of my energy. In every picture there are fragments of the world I knew. All my work is the pure expression of my passionate emotion in the face of nature and human beings. Anyone who looks carefully at my paintings and reads my correspondence will understand.

Years	The Life of Vincent van Gogh
1853–1857	1853 Born on March 30 in Groot Zundert, Holland. 1857 On May 1 his brother Theo is born.
1862–1869	1862 First animal drawings. 1864 Studies French, English, and German in the Zevenbergen school. 1869 Finishes school and works as an apprentice at Goupil and Company, art dealers.
1872–1877	1872 Spends lots of time with his brother Theo and begins their exchange of letters. 1873 Is transferred to the London gallery of Goupil and Company First love and first sketches of the city in letters to Theo. 1876 After a few months in the Paris gallery, he quits his job. Teacher in Ramsgate, England, and then in Isleworth, where he is also assistant pastor. 1877 Spends a few months working as a bookseller in Dordrecht, Holland. Devoted reader of the Bible.
1878–1883	1878 Takes a course in preaching. Draws mining families. Copies paintings by Millet. 1880 Formal anatomy and perspective studies at the academy of Brussels. Theo begins his economic and moral support of Vincent. 1881 Learns painting in The Hague with Anton van Rappard and Anton Mauve. 1882 Lives with Sien and her children. Begins painting in oils. 1883 Paints 250 pictures in Neunen. Develops a taste for portraits and self-portraits.
1884–1889	1884 Paints country life in the Brabant region. 1885 Paints *The Potato Eaters*. In March his father dies. 1886 After a few months in Antwerp, he goes to live with Theo in Paris. He meets the Impressionists: Pissarro, Monet, Renoir, Degas, Seurat. 1887 Studies in Cormon's workshop. Spends time with other artists in the cafés of Paris. 1888 Goes to Arles on February 20. Paints *The Yellow House* and *The Painter's Apartment*. Shares living quarters with Gauguin for two months. Violent argument and first major nervous breakdown. Vincent cuts off part of one ear. 1889 After recovering from his breakdown, paints the *Sunflowers* series. Voluntarily moves into the St. Paul-de-Mausolé asylum in Saint-Rémy. Paints *Starry Night* and *Irises*.
1890–1891	1890 Theo sells the first of Vincent's paintings, and the journalist Albert Aurier praises Vincent. The painter lives in Auvers-sur-Oise under the care of Dr. Gachet. Paints the doctor's portrait, several cypresses, and the church in Auvers-sur-Oise. On July 27 Vincent shoots himself in the stomach; he dies on July 29, 1890. 1891 Vincent's brother Theo dies on January 21.
1914–1931	1914 The two brothers finally lie together in the cemetery at Auvers-sur-Oise. 1931 Creation of the Vincent van Gogh Foundation in Amsterdam. His nephew Vincent donates all works, letters, and art collections that his father had been keeping for that purpose.

History		Art		Culture	
History		**Art**		**Culture**	
885	Universal Exposition in Paris	1855	*Painter's Study* by Courbet	1859	Darwin's Theory of Evolution
		1857	Millet's *The Sowers*		
861–1865	American Civil War	1859	Birth of Seurat	1865	Mendel formulates laws of heredity.
869	Vatican Council I in Rome	1863	Manet's *Le Déjeuner sur l'herbe*		
		1868	Impressionists' Salon		
872	First International in London	1874	First Impressionist exhibit. *Le Moulin de la Galette* by Renoir. *Impression: Rising Sun* by Monet.	1875	Georges Bizet composes the opera *Carmen*.
872	International Congress of The Hague			1876	Alexander Graham Bell invents the telephone.
873	First Spanish republic	1876	Second Impressionist exhibit; *The Absinthe Drinker* by Degas; *Nana* by Manet	1877	Edison invents the phonograph.
875	French Constitution				
877	Russian-Turkish War				
880	Boer War in South Africa	1880	Rodin's *Thinker*	1878	Birth of dancer Isadora Duncan
882	Triple Alliance among Germany, Austria-Hungary, and Italy	1881	Birth of Pablo Picasso; Renoir's *The Theater Box*	1879	Edison invents the electric lightbulb.
		1882	Birth of Georges Braque	1879	Siemens's electric locomotive
883	First Social Security laws in England	1882	*Self-Portrait* by Edvard Munch	1882	*Parsifal* by Richard Wagner
				1883	Death of Karl Marx
885	Creation of Belgian Congo	1883	Gaudi begins the *Holy Family* in Barcelona.	1884	Waterman invents the fountain pen.
886	Birth and reign of Alphonse XIII of Spain	1884	First independent salon	1885	*Thus Spake Zarathustra* by Nietsche
887	Dissolving of Reichstag	1886	Last Impressionist salon	1887	Hertz discovers electromagnetic waves.
888	Universal Exposition in Barcelona	1886	Birth of Mies van der Rohe	1888	Rimsky-Korsakov composes *Scheherazade*.
889	Universal Exposition in Paris	1886	*The Kiss*, sculpture by Rodin	1889	Birth of Charlie Chaplin
889	Second International in Paris	1887	*The Circus* by Seurat		
890	Bismarck deposed in Germany	1890	Exposition of Pont Aven School in the Voplini Café	1890	Dunlop invents the pneumatic tire.
891	Renewal of Triple Alliance; International Tribunal of The Hague	1891	First Nabi Exposition	189	Sir Arthur Conan Doyle creates the detective Sherlock Holmes.
		1897	*Whence Do We Come?* by Paul Gauguin		
900	Death of England's Queen Victoria	1900	*Water Lilies* by Monet	1892	Invention of Diesel engine
				1895	The Lumiére brothers invent motion pictures.
914–1918	World War I	1901	Van Gogh retrospective	1901	*Theory of Psychoanalysis* by Sigmund Freud
929	Creation of Vatican City within Rome	1929	Inauguration of MoMA in New York with the Cézanne, Gauguin, Seurat, and van Gogh exhibit	1913	Einstein's *General Theory of Relativity*

My name is...

is a collection of biographies of well-known people for young readers. In each book, a figure from history, science, art, culture, literature, or philosophy writes in an appealing way about his or her life and work, and about the world in which he or she lived. Abundant illustrations, inspired by the historical time period help us become immersed in the time and the environment.

Vincent van Gogh

Groot-Zundert

A native of the little Dutch town of Groot-Zundert, Vincent van Gogh was raised amid the strictness of his father, a Protestant minister, and his mother's kindness and love of nature. With a complex and unstable personality, in a few short years Vincent produced one of the most original and valuable bodies of painting of all time. His preoccupations and artistic techniques are reflected in the correspondence that he exchanged for years with his devoted brother Theo: light, color, line, subjects, his impressions and hallucinations... everything was recorded for eternity.